Starting His Way

Written and Illustrated by
Ron and Rebekah Coriell

Fleming H. Revell Company
Old Tappan, New Jersey

© 1981 Fleming H. Revell Company
All rights reserved
Printed in the United States of America

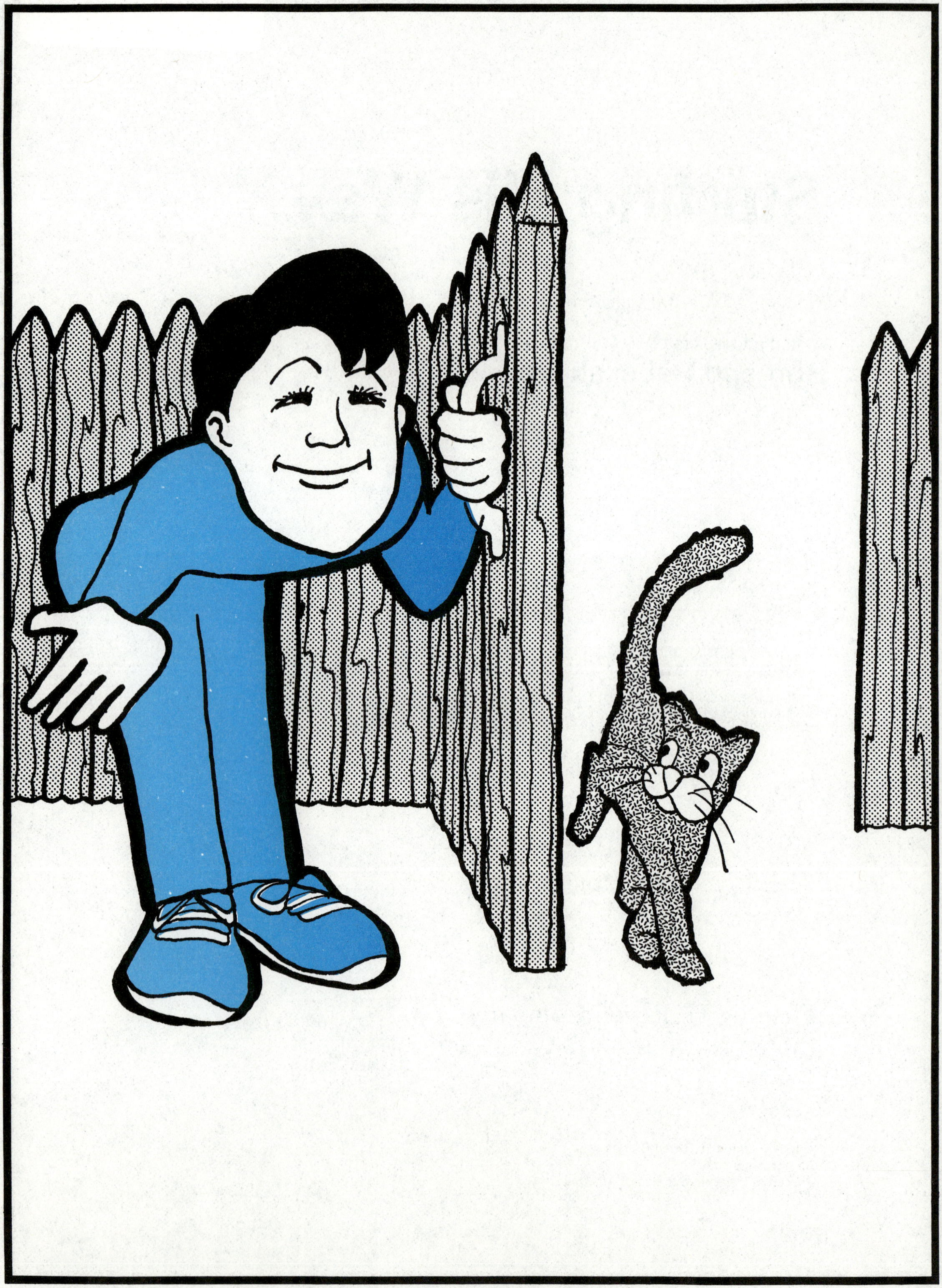

Initiate
gate

Making the First Move Without Being Asked

> Go to the ant, thou sluggard; consider her ways, and be wise: Which having no guide, overseer, or ruler, Provideth her meat in the summer, and gathereth her food in the harvest.
> Proverbs 6:6-8

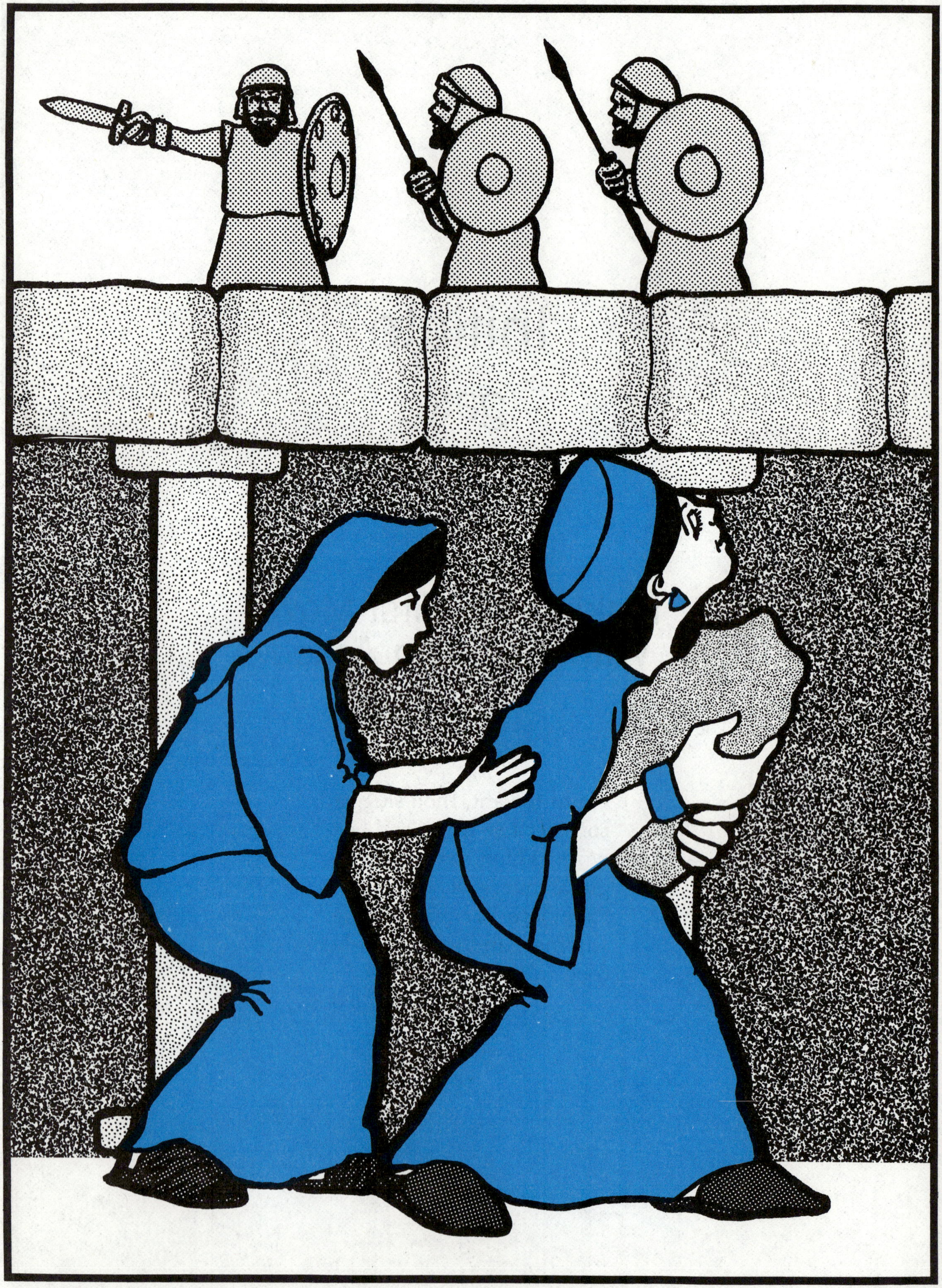

Initiative
in the Bible

The land of Israel reeled in turmoil. The blood of the royal families of Israel and Judah flowed freely. King Jehoram of Israel and King Ahaziah of Judah were killed on the same day by a general in the army of Israel. General Jehu then commanded his officers to go and collect the heads of King Jehoram's seventy brothers.

Meanwhile, the queen mother, Athalia, received the news of the death of her son, King Ahaziah. Most mothers would grieve with a broken heart, but not Athalia. She was as wicked as her mother, Jezebel. In bitterness she commanded that all the heirs to the throne of Judah be slain. It didn't matter that these were her own grandchildren.

In the midst of all of the wickedness was a godly woman named Jehosheba. She was the wife of a priest named Jehoiada. As the soldiers of Athalia ransacked the palace in search of royal heirs, Jehosheba sensed the danger that threatened her favorite nephew, named Joash. Although he was an infant, he was a grandson of the evil queen and therefore subject to being killed. With initiative she took him and his nurse and hid them in a bedchamber at the palace. Screams of pain and death echoed throughout the halls and surrounding rooms. But God, overshadowing these fugitives, did not allow the soldiers to find them. Jehosheba then removed them from the palace and hid them in a room in the Temple of God.

For the next six years, Athalia ruled the land. The worship of the idol Baal was more firmly entrenched into the religious life of the land of Judah. All this time young Joash was raised by his godly aunt and uncle and trained in the worship of the true God, Jehovah. Joash's presence in the Temple was secure because wicked Athalia had no reason to go there.

Jehoiada patiently waited for God's timing. He knew that circumstances must be just right before he could reveal the rightful king to the nation.

When Joash was seven years old, his uncle knew that the people of Judah were distressed with the ruthless rule of Athalia. They were ripe for revolution. Exercising initiative, he summoned various civil, religious, and military authorities to meet with him at the Temple. They obeyed him because he was the high priest and his office commanded the respect of the people. Upon their coming, he swore them to secrecy and introduced them to Joash, the rightful king of Judah. The men were surprised to see that an heir still lived. Each man pledged his loyalty to Joash.

Jehoiada then ordered that these men serve as guards.

"And he commanded them, saying, 'This is the thing that ye shall do: A third part of you that enter in on the sabbath shall even be keepers of the watch of the king's house; And a third part shall be at the gate of Sur; and a third part at the gate behind the guard: so shall ye keep the watch of the house, that it be not broken down" (2 Kings 11:5, 6).

Then Jehoiada commanded that the priests who served on the Sabbath day be personal bodyguards of Joash. To arm them, Jehoiada opened the armory at the Temple and issued spears and shields that had been King David's.

"And ye shall compass the king round about, every man with his weapons in his hand: and he that cometh within the ranges, let him be slain: and be ye with the king as he goeth out and as he cometh in" (2 Kings 11:8).

On the Sabbath, in great ceremony, young Joash was brought before the people gathered in the Temple. A wave of amazement swept through the crowd at the revealing of the new young king. The royal crown was brought forth for the rightful king of Judah.

Instantly the people showed their acceptance of their new ruler by clapping their hands. They shouted, "God save the king" (2 Kings 11:12).

From the palace, Queen Athalia heard the joyous roar of the people. Out of curiosity she attired herself and went to the Temple to see what was happening.

As she strode proudly into the great room, almost no one noticed her. Great was the rejoicing and sound of the trumpets. Then she discovered Joash, clothed in the regalia of the king of Judah.

Tearing her clothes, she cried, "Treason! Treason!" (2 Kings 11:14). Then she turned and ran out of the Temple.

Jehoiada quickly commanded his guards to kill her. In reverence to the holiness of the Temple, the guards did not overtake her there.

Athalia tried to escape through the horse stalls, into the back door of the palace. Before she could reach safety, she was killed by a pursuing Temple guard. Thus ended the bloody reign of the wicked queen Athalia.

Jehoiada made a covenant between the Lord, King Joash, and the people, that they should serve Him with all their hearts. The altars of Baal were broken down, and Baal's high priest was slain. Then all the people of the land of Judah rejoiced, and seven-year-old Joash began his reign as king.

The Lord used a godly aunt and uncle to save a young king in the midst of bloody turmoil. Their initiative in a time of crisis encouraged others to stand alone.

The story of Jehosheba is taken from 2 Kings 9:24-11:16 and 2 Chronicles 22:8-23:15.

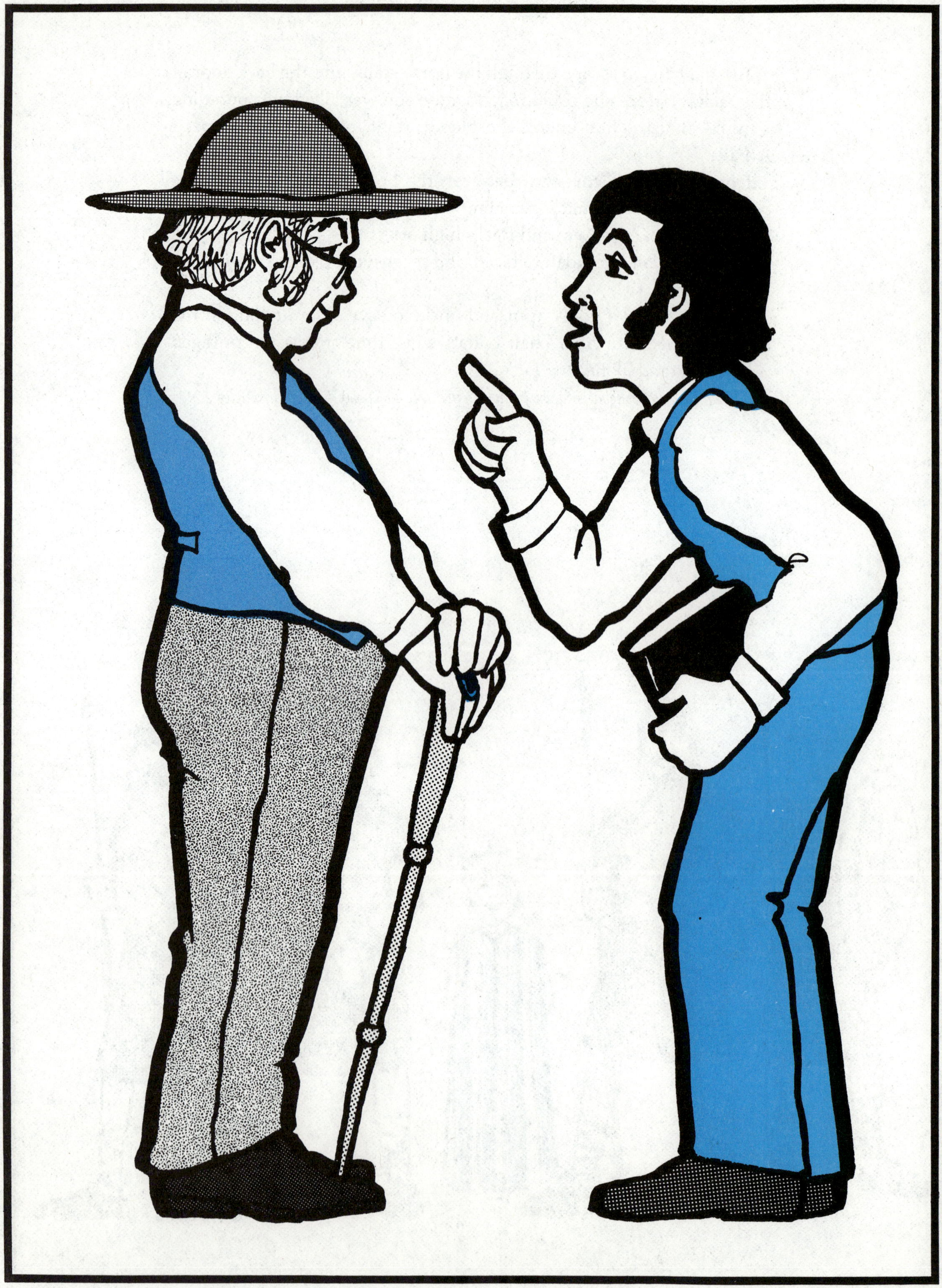

Initiative
of a Hero of the Faith

Bill Knibb had a good job as a printer. He was very happy, until one day in 1822 two Baptist ministers entered the printshop. Bill greeted both men, for he knew them well.

"We have news from Jamaica about your brother," they said.

Bill left his press. Three months earlier, his brother had gone to Jamaica to do missionary work among the slaves of that Caribbean island. Bill was aware that the slave owners were opposed to missionaries.

Dr. Ryland hesitated and then said, "We have come to tell you, Bill, that your brother is dead. He died of a fever."

"Oh, no, no!" he protested. "Not Tom! It couldn't be! Tom was so good! Tom was doing such a great work for God!" At length, Bill stopped weeping. Softly he said, "Don't worry, Tom. I'm going to carry on your work for you."

Taking the initiative, William turned to the ministers and boldly proclaimed, "I'll go to Jamaica to take Tom's place."

Dr. Ryland smiled at William Knibb and said, "I am sure the missionary society will send you, Bill. And God will bless your mission."

William left the printshop to go to school and train to be a teacher. He also married a girl from his church. In 1824 they set sail for Jamaica as missionaries.

Upon their arrival, it didn't take them long to discern the oppression of the suffering slaves. He wrote his mother about slavery, "I feel a burning hatred against it as one of the most odious monsters that ever disgraced the earth."

As he visited the school where his brother, Tom, had taught, Bill was distressed to see it almost wrecked. He erected a new school that served 250 black children. William continued to build schools across the island. He organized the Christian slaves into the Jamaica Baptist Association in 1826.

William Knibb realized that only if the slaves were freed would they be able to worship and work in peace. Thus William exercised initiative by beginning a campaign against slavery on the island.

His declarations from the pulpit that slavery was indecent and unchristian were scorned and ridiculed by the rich landowners. Then the newspapers published lies about him and his fellow missionaries. Even the magistrate of Kingston, Jamaica, tried to persuade him to keep quiet.

"I am sent here to preach," the missionary replied, "and preach I must." In public meetings the slaveowners denounced William Knibb and his associates as "lunatics." And at last the slavery forces succeeded in getting William arrested and placed in jail.

During his imprisonment, schools and churches were wrecked and burned. Slaves were threatened and their homes destroyed. A law was passed prohibiting the work of Mr. Knibb and his mission.

After being freed from jail in 1832, William returned to England. He immediately met with the executive committee of the missionary society. They advised him to keep silent.

William Knibb responded, "We have landed here without a shilling. But if necessary, I will take my wife and children by the hand, and I will walk barefoot throughout the length and breadth of the United Kingdom. We will make known to the Christians of England what their brethren in Jamaica are suffering."

For the next two years, William Knibb waged a one-man campaign against the shackles of slavery. He spoke at schools, churches, and at public rallies. So zealous were his eloquent words that vast numbers of people began to side with him. Soon the English Parliament began to feel the pressure. A bill to abolish slavery was hotly debated and passed. July 31, 1833 was set as the day when colonial slavery would be abolished in the British Empire. At Mr. Knibb's insistence, Parliament also agreed to pay a large sum of restitution money so that churches, schools, and homes could be repaired and rebuilt in Jamaica.

William Knibb hurried to Jamaica so that he could be with the slaves when they were freed. It was a grand celebration. As the clock struck midnight on the appointed day, Mr. Knibb said, "The cruel monster is dead! The Negro is free! Thanks be to God!"

William Knibb's initiative to take his brother Tom's place as a missionary resulted in the spiritual freedom of thousands in Jamaica. And his initiative to fight the curse of slavery physically freed millions across the British Empire.

Character Development Challenges

Crossword Puzzle—Initiative

ACROSS

1. _____ went to Rome to search for Paul and encourage him. 2 Timothy 1:16, 17
5. _____ entertained three strangers. Genesis 18:1-8
7. _____ rescued Jeremiah from a dungeon. Jeremiah 38:7-13
9. _____ got David a drink of water from a well in enemy territory. 2 Samuel 23:15-18
10. _____ anointed Jesus' feet. John 12:3
12. _____ killed a Canaanite general. Judges 4:21
13. _____ saved young King Joash's life. 2 Kings 11:2
14. _____ brought God the firstlings of his flock. Genesis 4:4
16. _____ used an ox goad to kill 600 Philistines. Judges 3:31
18. _____ rebuilt the walls around Jerusalem. Nehemiah 2:5
19. _____ offered to draw water for the camels of Abraham's servant. Genesis 24:15-19
20. _____ opened her home in Philippi so that Paul could stay there. Acts 16:14, 15
21. _____ went to Pilate and asked him for the body of Jesus. Matthew 27:57, 58

DOWN

2. _____ entertained Elisha. 2 Kings 4:8-12
3. _____ befriended David when he was fleeing from Absalom. 2 Samuel 17:27, 28
4. _____ moved a well lid to help a woman water her flock of sheep. Genesis 29:10
6. Paul's _____ warned him of a plot to take his life. Acts 23:16
8. _____ fought a giant. 1 Samuel 17:32
11. _____ saved David's life. 2 Samuel 21:17
12. King _____ repaired the temple. 2 Kings 22:3-7
13. _____ offered to take the blame if he did not return his brother to his father. Genesis 43:8
15. _____ befriended Paul and introduced him to the apostles. Acts 9:26, 27
17. _____ found the boy with two fish and five barley loaves. John 6:8, 9

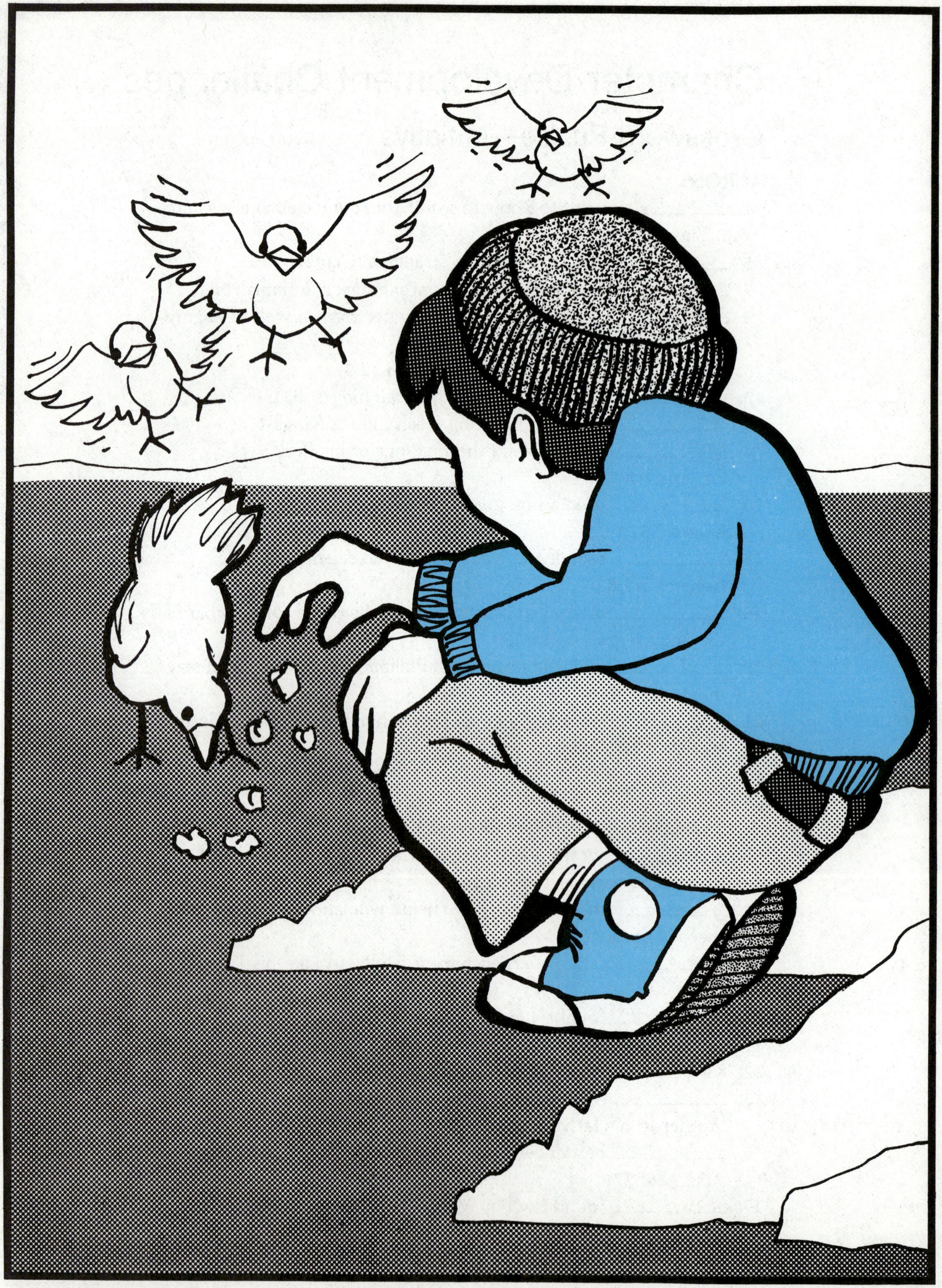

Love
dove

Meeting Another's Need Unselfishly

This is my commandment,
That ye love one another, as
I have loved you.
                    John 15:12

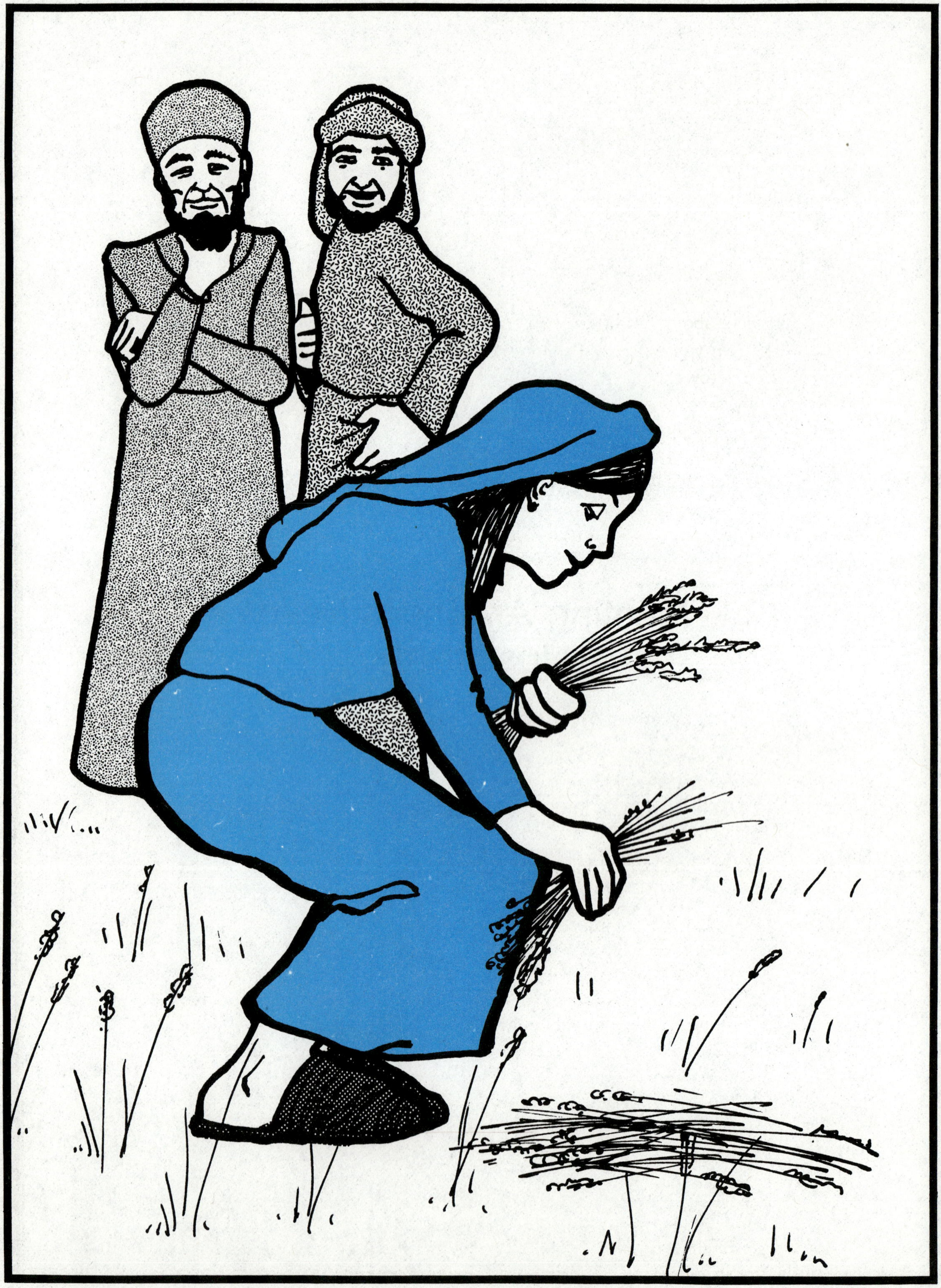

Love
in the Bible

Ruth buried her head on the shoulder of her mother-in-law, Naomi. Each wept because of the grief that she felt. Death had claimed their beloved husbands, and they were now alone. How could God possibly bring about good from such misery?

Ten years before, Naomi and her husband, Elimelech, had left their hometown of Bethlehem because of a famine in the land. They took their two sons, crossed the Jordan river, and settled in the land of Moab, among the descendants of Lot, Abraham's nephew. There they were able to make a living and raise their family.

Then the second trial came upon them: Elimelech died. A grieving Naomi was left with her two sons. Each boy soon married, and Naomi once again was joyful. Her new daughters-in-law were named Orpah and Ruth. Both were Moabites. Before they could bear any children, death struck the household again and claimed both sons. Now Naomi was truly alone.

Upon hearing that food was available in the land of Israel, Naomi decided to return to Bethlehem, where she owned property. She encouraged Orpah and Ruth to stay behind in their homeland. Perhaps they would be able to find husbands.

Orpah decided to stay in Moab. Yet Ruth, whose name means "friendship," would not consent to leave Naomi.

"And Ruth said, 'Intreat me not to leave thee, or to return from following after thee: for whither thou goest, I will go; and where thou lodgest, I will lodge: thy people shall be my people, and thy God my God. Where thou diest, will I die, and there will I be buried ...'" (Ruth 1:16, 17).

Naomi could not resist Ruth's love. It was a self-sacrificing love. It meant that Ruth was willing to give up her homeland, her friends, and her god, Chemosh. It was also a self-giving love that promised to meet the needs of her mother-in-law. So the two returned to Bethlehem.

It was the beginning of the barley harvest when they arrived. They were without money or food. Therefore Ruth offered to go unto the fields and gather the stalks of grain left by the reapers. Whatever was left in the fields was reserved for the poorest of the people. Out of love, Ruth was willing to humble herself.

God led her to a field that belonged to a wealthy Jew named Boaz. He was a kind and generous man who willingly allowed the poor to glean in his fields. Upon seeing Ruth, he asked his workers about her and learned her name. He had heard about her because of her reputation for love for Naomi, which had spread among the neighbors.

Boaz spoke kindly to Ruth and said, "Go not to glean in another field, neither go from hence, but abide here fast by my maidens... have I not charged the young men that they shall not touch thee? And when thou art thirsty, go unto the vessels, and drink of that which the young men have drawn" (Ruth 2:8, 9).

Ruth was overwhelmed by the generous spirit of this stranger. Prejudice was strong, especially that of the Jews against Moabites. Ruth bowed herself to the ground in humble gratefulness.

Boaz continued, "At mealtime come thou hither, and eat of the bread, and dip thy morsel in the vinegar" (Ruth 2:14).

This was a gracious favor Boaz offered her. He allowed her to partake of the common bowl of food that he provided for his workers. Ruth must have sensed that here was a man who, like herself, loved to meet the needs of others.

In order to insure that Ruth gathered enough grain, Boaz instructed his reapers to drop handfuls on purpose. Ruth was able to take home a good amount of grain.

Naomi and Ruth's needs were met throughout the harvest seasons as Ruth made frequent trips to glean in Boaz' fields.

Naomi's love for her daughter-in-law prompted thoughts about a suitable husband for her. Boaz was Naomi's relative. Eastern custom stated that the nearest relative of a widow had the right to buy her property and marry her daughter. Therefore Naomi set in motion a plan to help Ruth marry Boaz.

In the summer the men would glean in the day and thresh the grain from late afternoon until sunset, when it was cooler. Then they would make their beds next to their pile of grain to insure that robbers did not steal it. This was Boaz' practice.

Naomi instructed Ruth to wash, anoint herself with perfume, and put on beautiful raiment. Then she was to go down to the place where Boaz was threshing and wait until after he had finished his late evening meal and had retired for the night. Quietly she was to go to him, uncover his feet, and lie down at the foot of his bed. Then she was to wait until he woke up and told her what to do. This strange Eastern custom was a way of asking for a man's protection in marriage.

When Boaz awakened in the night and beheld Ruth at his feet, his heart went out to her. Lovingly he agreed to marry her if one obstacle could be cleared. He was not the nearest relative. Therefore he would first have to offer the sale of the property and the marriage of Ruth to the other relative.

On the next day Boaz went to the gate of the city, where legal matters were discussed. He met the nearest relative there and gathered ten city elders to hear the case. The matter was discussed, and the man refused to marry Ruth. To seal the agreement, he took off his sandal and handed it to Boaz. Boaz held it up over his head so that all could be witnesses. This symbolized that the nearest relative would never walk on Naomi's land as its owner.

Boaz happily purchased the property of Naomi and married Ruth, whom he loved.

God indeed turned sorrow into joy for Naomi. Ruth's love for her mother-in-law earned her the respect and then the love of Boaz. The first child born to them became the grandfather of the greatest king of Israel: David. And 1,100 years later, a child was born in Bethlehem, a descendant of Boaz and Ruth. His name was Jesus.

The story is taken from the Book of Ruth.

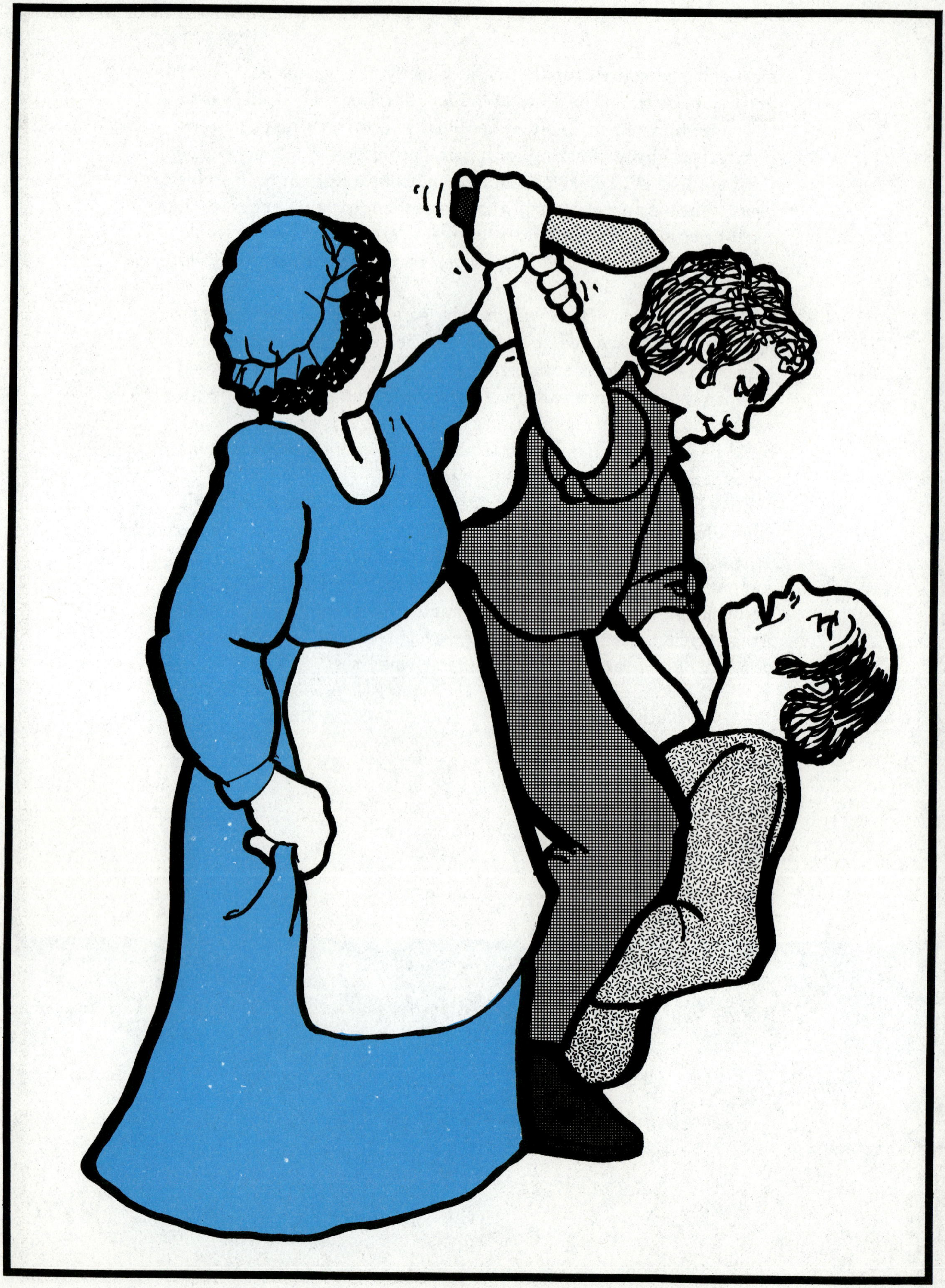

Love
of a Hero of the Faith

As the stout woman made her way through the streets of Elberfeld, Germany, flocks of raggedly dressed children ran to meet her. She sang to them, spoke words of encouragement, and gave them some used clothing. Hanna Faust was on another of her daily mercy missions.

Aunt Hanna, as she was called, was a coffee peddler by trade. She carried large baskets under each arm, from which she sold Java and Mocha coffees. She was a Christian who wanted to give God's love to others. She did this by attempting to meet the needs of others.

As a girl, Hanna had felt called by God to love others in very practical ways. After working all day in a weaving mill, she would use her evenings to visit the sick and the poor. She would sweep rooms, make beds, and scrub down the filthiest of floors.

In 1840 the ravages of disease swept through Europe. Hanna had the symptoms of cholera, but she continued her labors of love. Trusting the Lord for better health, Hanna prayed, "Lord, You cannot really take me away from my poor sick ones; they need me too sorely." God responded by miraculously preserving her. While hundreds died of cholera, typhus, and smallpox, Hanna Faust worked to aid the dying.

Her coffee trade brought her into the homes of the wealthy. It was nothing for them to give away the clothing that had gone out of style from one month to another. Hanna was glad to receive these secondhand things and give them to the poor. The bakers in town gave her bread that was too dry to sell. Many starving families were kept alive by Hanna's bread deliveries.

In all her good deeds of love, Hanna shared the Gospel. An example was her ministry to a group of East Prussian emigrants who lived in huts outside of Elberfeld.

Hanna began to invite the emigrant children to a Sunday school she was planning. So many came that a barn was used to contain the crowd. Finally, with the help of Christians in Elberfeld, a special building was erected. As people were saved, Christian unions for men were organized.

Hanna's great love for people created in her a boldness that often exposed her to danger. On her way to call a doctor, her path took her through dark and dangerous streets. Suddenly some tough boys jumped in front of her and threatened to hurt her. Fearlessly Hanna looked them in the eyes and said, "Look fellows, I just came from the bed of a dying woman. I'm on my way to get a doctor, and nothing is going to stop me, not even you!" Then she witnessed to them about death, judgment, eternity, and God's love.

Hanna also was a testimony for Christ in the wealthy homes that she visited while selling coffee. The rich young girls would look forward to her coming. They sensed her love and willingly shared their problems with Hanna, who had an understanding spirit.

Factory girls also confided in Hanna and asked for instruction in Christian ways. Hanna could relate well to them because she had worked in factories when she was younger.

Once, as Hanna was sitting in a meeting, she was startled by an inner voice that seemed to tell her to go home. *Why should I go home?* she thought. But the inner urging continued so strongly that at last she got up and ran home. When she reached the street in front of her house, Hanna found a group of men clustered around two others who were fighting. So strong was Hanna's love for people that she did not think twice. Using her hefty weight, she pushed her way into the center of the ring of men. She was just in time to seize the arm of a man who was about to plunge a knife into his father's heart. The she rebuked the onlookers and took the son to his house, witnessing to him all the way.

City officials said that Hanna was worth a squad of policemen. The street railway even furnished her with a life long free pass.

When Hanna died in 1903, hundreds followed her funeral procession, with mounted police leading the way. People thronged to their windows to catch a last glimpse of Aunt Hanna. Hanna Faust never was rich in this world's goods, but she was rich in her love toward others.

Character Development Challenges

Who Can I Love and How?

Meeting another's need is the essence of love. Below are references that give scriptural guidelines about love. In the spaces provided, list people whom you can love and tell how you can accomplish this in a practical way.

References	Love Defined	Whom I Can Love	How I Can Love
1 Corinthians 13:4	is kind	my brother	read to him
1 Peter 3:9	not revengeful	my enemy	do him good
1 Corinthians 13:4	suffers long		
1 Corinthians 13:4	envies not		
1 Corinthians 13:4	boasts not		
1 Corinthians 13:4	is not puffed up		
1 Corinthians 13:5	behaves itself		
1 Corinthians 13:5	seeks welfare of others		
1 Corinthians 13:5	remains calm		
1 Corinthians 13:5	pure minded		
1 Corinthians 13:6	sad about sin		
1 Corinthians 13:6	rejoices in truth		
1 Corinthians 13:7	bears all things		
1 Corinthians 13:7	believes all things		
1 Corinthians 13:7	hopes all things		
1 Corinthians 13:7	endures all things		
Galatians 5:13	serves others		
Romans 13:10	fulfills the law		
1 Peter 1:22	is pure		
1 Peter 3:8	is courteous		
1 Peter 4:8	covers many sins		

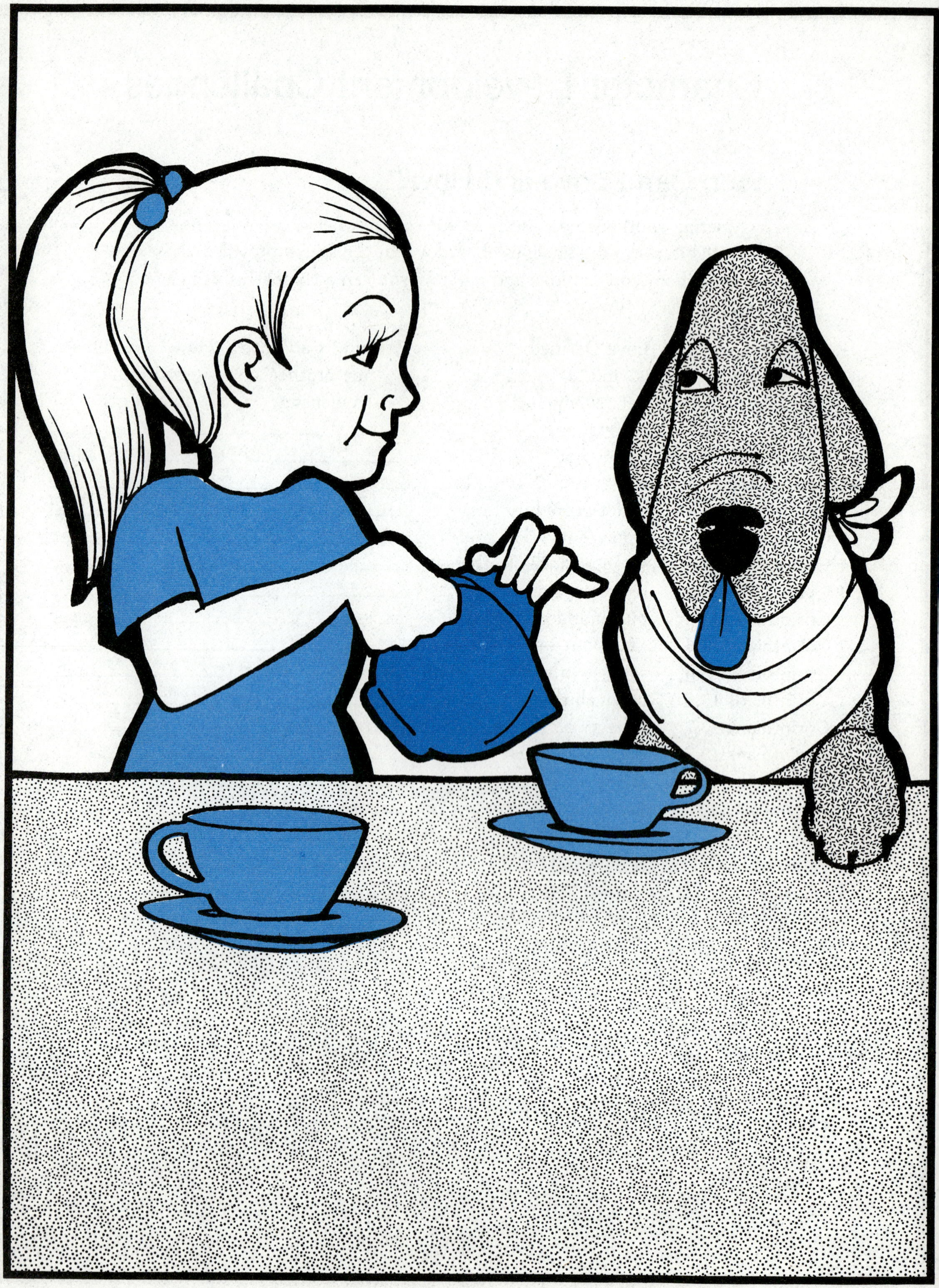

Generosity
tea

Sharing What I Have With a Happy Spirit

Every man according as he purposeth in his heart, so let him give; not grudgingly, or of necessity: for God loveth a cheerful giver.
                    2 Corinthians 9:7

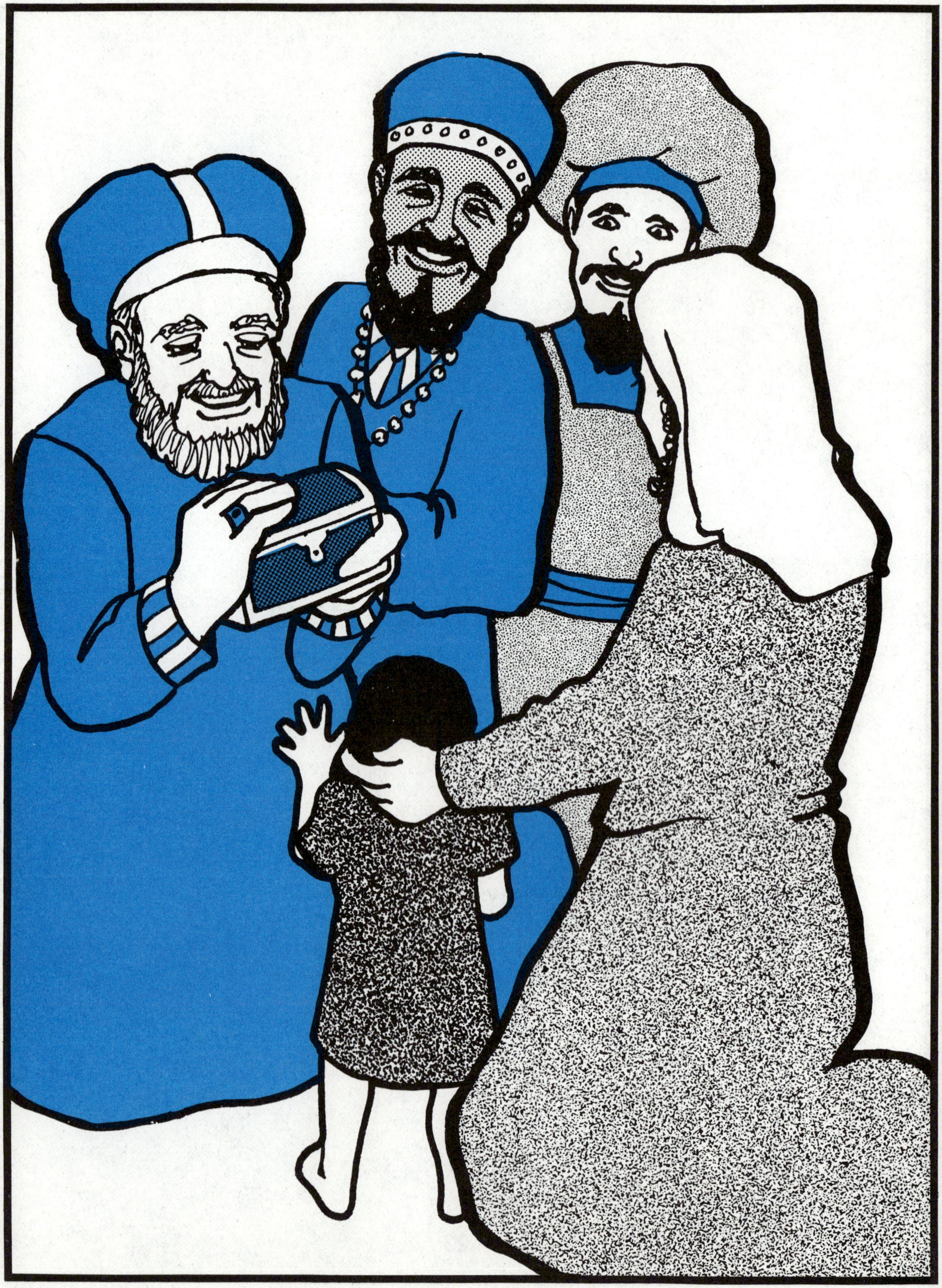

Generosity
in the Bible

People from Jerusalem hurried to witness the unusual sight. Rarely did such a caravan enter their city. It consisted of many servants and nobles dressed in elaborate garments. With them were many animals carrying baggage. At the head of the line was a group of richly dressed men who appeared to be of high rank.

As the caravan weaved its way through the city, word spread to the palace of Herod the Great. Upon hearing a description of these visitors, he decided to greet them personally. Perhaps they bore gifts for him or came to ask his advice.

Herod was a talented yet evil tyrant. He had been appointed the ruler of Judea by the Romans, thirty-five years earlier. He had promoted an elaborate building program in Jerusalem, which included rebuilding the Temple. Yet Herod was so suspicious and jealous that he killed members of his immediate family, including his wife and his favorite son, when he felt they were disloyal.

With pride he received the group of wealthy visitors. Upon questioning them, he found that they were magi—magicians who were priests from Persia. They were advisers to their king and studied astrology, astronomy, medicine, and worshiped the elements such as fire, air, earth, and water. They also were familiar with the Jewish Scriptures.

They asked Herod, "Where is He that is born King of the Jews? for we have seen His star in the east, and are come to worship Him" (Matthew 2:2).

Herod's expression changed greatly at these words. It troubled him that such important and learned men were seeking a king in his area. Would this new king rival his rule?

Soon all Jerusalem knew the mission of the magi. They were troubled because they feared a cruel reaction by Herod. A short time before this, some Pharisees had predicted that the descendants of one of Herod's relatives would inherit his throne. In anger Herod had rashly put these Pharisees to death. Would his jealousy again cause him to react violently?

Herod quickly ordered all the chief priests and scribes to assemble before him. Then he demanded to know where the Messiah of the Jews would be born. The Old Testament Scripture was well-known to these men. They quoted the verse in Micah 5:2: "Bethleham Ephratah, though thou be little among the thousands of Judah, yet out of thee shall he come forth unto me that is to be ruler in Israel."

This confirmed Herod's fears. Taking the magi aside, he inquired about the exact time the star had appeared. Such an event was thought to signal the occurrence of an important event. Perhaps this was when this Messiah had been born.

The magi explained that the star had appeared two years earlier. It was then that they had decided to travel the thousand miles to Jerusalem to discover the king. They had come bringing gifts for Him and desiring to worship Him.

Herod's evil mind conceived a plan that would result in his rival's death. He encouraged the magi to go directly to Bethlehem and to search diligently for the child-king.

"And when ye have found Him," said Herod, "bring me word again, that I may come and worship Him also" (Matthew 2:8).

Bethlehem was a small town about five miles south of Jerusalem. As the magi began their journey, they rejoiced to see the star guiding them.

The magi felt a great sense of anticipation. This was the moment they had awaited. They were at last ready to see the future King.

They had not come empty-handed. Being men of great wealth, they had brought gifts to generously bestow upon the child. One gift was gold. Another gift was frankincense, a gum obtained from the bark of a special tree. The third gift, myrrh, was used for perfume, to improve the taste of wine, and to be an ingredient of a very precious ointment.

Common men could not afford such expensive gifts. However, the magi were uncommon in their vast wealth as well as in their generosity.

Upon entering the house in Bethlehem, they were surprised to find a humble family. There was no throne, no elaborate decor, and no regally dressed attendants. Mary and Joseph looked up in wonder at the sight of these visitors. Until now, shepherds had been their only visitors. Could it be that these strangers had come to the wrong house?

The magi were certain of the position of the star. There could be no mistake that this was the house. Falling down upon their hands and knees, they humbly bowed before the babe and worshiped Him. Then they opened their gifts and gave them to Jesus.

By faith these men believed that the child was the fulfillment of the Old Testament prophecies. After making their presentation, they left, rejoicing that they had seen the Messiah.

As they slept that evening, before returning to Jerusalem, they were warned by God in a dream. They were told to avoid Herod and to return to Persia by an alternate route.

That same night an angel appeared to Joseph in a dream and warned him to take his family to safety in Egypt. Herod, angry because the magi did not return to him, ordered that all the children of Bethlehem who were two years old and younger should be killed.

The generosity of the magi was threefold. They had given two years of their *time* to search for the Messiah. They had given of their *labors* to travel many weary miles to find Him. And they had generously given of their *wealth* in gold, frankincense, and myrrh.

The story of the magi is taken from Matthew 2.

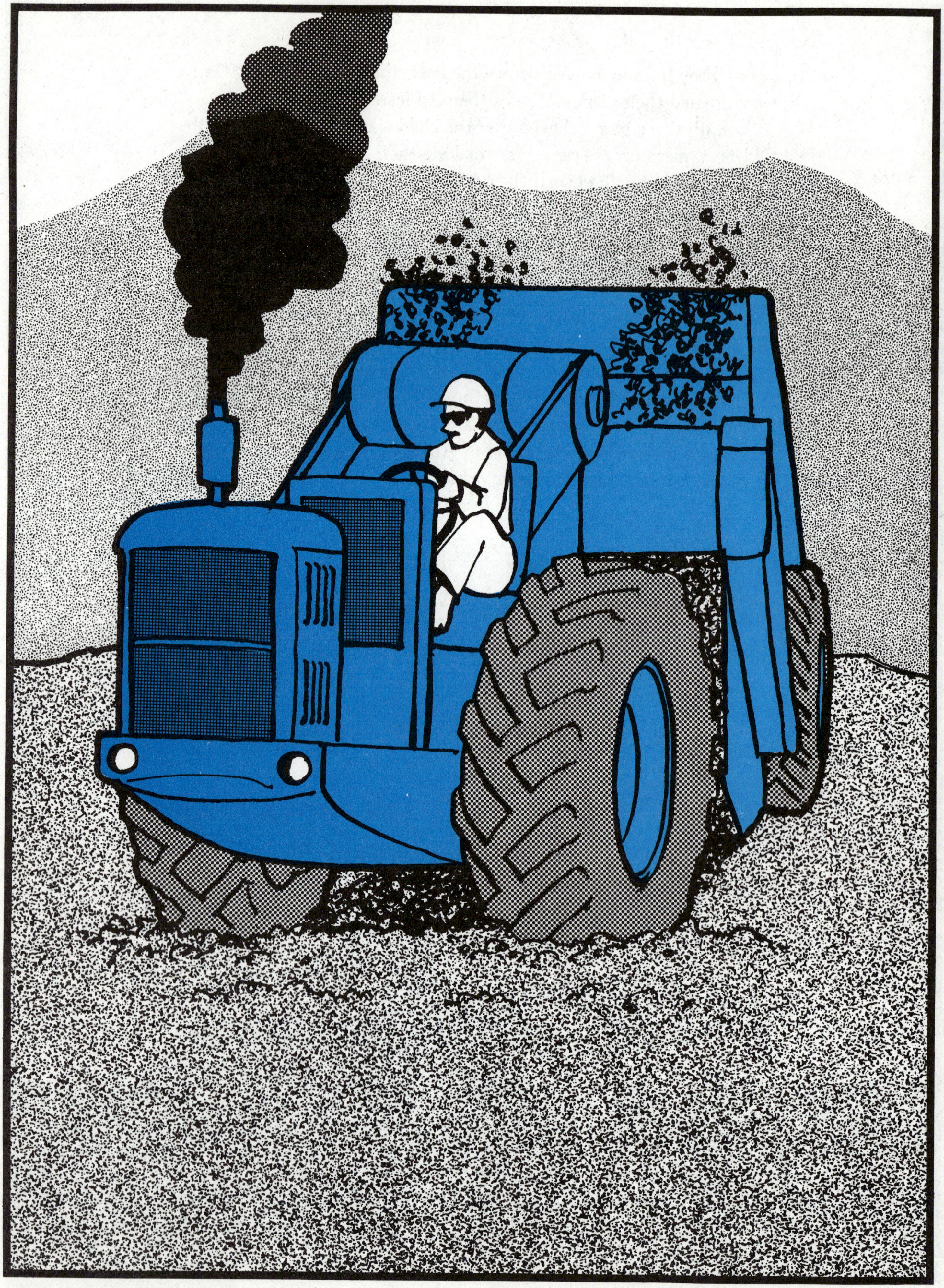

Generosity
of a Hero of the Faith

With a roar, the huge machines belched out billows of black smoke and lurched forward. Shaking and tearing the ground in their fury, they scooped tons of earth with their huge blades. One, two, three... eleven, twelve, and thirteen passed by. Each machine had the same name painted on its side: LeTourneau.

Robert LeTourneau was born in 1888 to Christian parents. He inherited his mechanical aptitude from his father and his enthusiasm from his mother. He was a boy with a strong body and powerful will. He was also impatient, ambitious, rebellious, imaginative, and talented beyond his years.

About the time he was sixteen, he began to realize that there was something missing in his life. God led him to attend special revival meetings. On the sixth night he gave his rebellious will to Christ and was saved.

During the next ten years Robert was married and had seven children. He learned a key skill that would affect the rest of his life.

In partnership with a friend, Mr. LeTourneau opened an auto-repair business. While repairing cars, Robert learned to weld. His creative mind invented a host of quicker and cheaper ways to make repairs.

After World War I, he found a job driving a tractor and pulling a primitive earthmover. He liked the work so much that he convinced a banker to loan him the cash so he could buy his own earthmover and tractor and become a contractor. Then he redesigned the earthmover so it would work more efficiently. He used welded steel to make it lighter, stronger, and cheaper.

Another contractor liked Mr. LeTourneau's new design so much that he bought it. Robert designed himself a new and better one with the profits. Then someone bought his new earthmover. Soon Mr. LeTourneau found himself building earthmovers and doing little contracting.

Yet as his business prospered, his spiritual life was aimless. He prayed, "Lord, if You will give me a victorious Christian life and put the love in my heart that I know ought to be there and fill me with Your Spirit so that I can witness for You, I'll do whatever You ask me to do from this day on." Later he added, "I will do my best to be God's businessman."

From the minute Robert LeTourneau made God his business partner, things really started to prosper. In the next twenty years, Mr. LeTourneau created numerous earthmoving machinery designs. He had to build three factories to handle the orders. It was amazing that during the depression, he became a millionaire.

The generosity of Robert LeTourneau began to become evident as his business grew bigger. On one occasion he struggled over whether to make his customary annual missionary pledge. Work had been slow, and he needed all available funds to keep the business going. At last he decided to pledge $5,000 and trust God to meet his needs. Soon thereafter he sold a new model of an earthmover to a contractor. The man liked it so much that he ordered another one.

"Wait a minute," replied Mr. LeTourneau. "I have only built one of those big scrapers."

The contractor then asked, "Well, can't you build another one?"

"Yes," he answered, "but I'm short of money. Could you give me a little down payment?"

"Down payment!" the contractor exclaimed. "I'll write you a check for the whole amount right now!"

Robert LeTourneau returned to his factory with a check for $25,000 in his pocket.

Not only was Mr. LeTourneau generous with his money, but he also freely gave of his time. One example was the night he had to design an important component for one of his huge machines. As he sat down to his drafting board, he remembered he had promised to go to a mission with the church's young people. Inwardly he struggled. His men needed the design the next day in order to manufacture the machine on time to meet a deadline. Yet he had promised the young people. Mr. LeTourneau went to the mission.

He returned late that night to resume his task of designing the important part. He hadn't been there long before the entire design flashed into his mind. In ten minutes he put it on paper and went to bed. That vital part of a control unit made LeTourneau earthmovers more advanced than all the competition and kept them that way for years.

Mr. LeTourneau further gave of his time by using his weekends to speak in churches, camps, and conventions all across the country. His thrilling Christian testimony was so much in demand that he had to buy a large passenger airplane to transport him and a Gospel team to all the meetings.

Perhaps Mr. LeTourneau's greatest generosity was evidenced when he decided to give God 98 percent of his income and only live on 2 percent. He established a nonprofit foundation with these funds. Millions of dollars were then available for God to use in all kinds of ministries that have furthered the Gospel.

Character Development Challenges

Generous Jumble

Hidden in the maze of letters below are the names of thirteen people in Scripture who were generous. Using the references at the bottom of the page, find each name and circle it.

```
A H A Z I A J B O A P A L
D A J O N A T H A N H I E
A B H J O B A D I A H H B
N A R O T N A S A L R L J
A R T A X E R X E S A Y O
B Z A H E S I B J A O D S
R I D A V I D E O B H I E
A L M S H P E Y S T L A P
H L A U A H I M E L E C H
A A C E B O A Z P E B A D
M I H R E R T A H B H Z L
E H I U T U J I T L E A H
B A R S O S A B E L I E S
```

Genesis 43:30-34   Genesis 45:16-20   Ruth 2:15-17
1 Samuel 30:21   1 Samuel 21:1-6   Esther 7:2; 1:1
1 Samuel 18:4   1 Kings 18:4   Nehemiah 2:1-8
2 Timothy 1:16   Acts 16:14, 15   Luke 23:50-53
Genesis 13:8, 9

Write out ways to be generous with the following:

Time _____
Possessions _____
Money _____
Praise _____
Talents _____

32